AMERICA IN THE 20TH CENTURY
(1913-1999)

TITLE LIST

AMERICA IN THE 20TH CENTURY

(1913-1999)

BY VICTOR SOUTH

MASON CREST

Mason Crest
370 Reed Road
Broomall, Pennsylvania 19008
www.masoncrest.com

Printed and bound in Hashemite Kingdom of Jordan.

First printing
9 8 7 6 5 4 3 2 1

Library of Congress Cataloging-in-Publication Data

South, Victor.
 America in the 20th century (1913-1999) / by Victor South.
    p. cm. — (How America became America)
 ISBN 978-1-4222-2408-3 (hardcover) — ISBN 978-1-4222-2396-3 (series hardcover) — ISBN 978-1-4222-9318-8 (ebook)
 1. United States—History—20th century—Juvenile literature. 2. United States—History, Military—20th century—Juvenile literature. 3. United States—Foreign relations—20th century—Juvenile literature. I. Title.
 E741.S66 2013
 973.91—dc23

                                    2012010412

Produced by Harding House Publishing Services, Inc.
www.hardinghousepages.com
Cover design by Torque Advertising + Design.

1914–World War I begins.

1919–The League of Nations is born, but the United States does not join.

1932–Franklin Delano Roosevelt becomes the president.

1918–World War I ends; the Allies win.

1931–Droughts in the Midwest cause the Dust Bowl.

1941–Japan bombs Pearl Harbor and the United States enters World War II.

1917–The United States joins World War I on the side of the Allies.

1945–World War II ends.

1939–Germany invades Poland and World War II begins.

1929–The stock market crashes and the Great Depression begins.

1945–The United Nations is born.

1950–The United States gets involved in the Korean War.

1968–Civil rights leader Martin Luther King, Jr. is assassinated.

2000–George W. Bush wins a close election against Al Gore.

1962–The Cuban Missile Crisis is avoided when the United States and the Soviet Union compromise.

1975–The Vietnam War ends after years of protest.

1955–The United States gets involved in the Vietnam War.

1974–Richard M. Nixon resigns as president.

2001–Terrorists attack the United States on September 11.

1963–President John F. Kennedy is assassinated.

1991–The Soviet Union dissolves and the Cold War is over.

Chapter One
WAR AND POWER

Today, the United States is the most powerful country in the world. It has the most economic power. It has the strongest army. It influences other countries' governments.

But that wasn't always true. Other places have been more powerful. And they were around a lot longer. Think of the Roman Empire long ago. It ruled for hundreds of years! The United States is still pretty young. The country is only about 250 years old. There are lots of countries that are much older! And the United States didn't always have so much power.

So how did it happen? How did this young nation get so much power in such a short period of time?

It happened mostly because of a war. World War I helped launch the United States into such a powerful position.

The word **economic** has to do with money. The economy of a country is everything that has to do with making money—jobs, businesses, factories, farms, banks. So when we say that the United States is an economic power, we mean that it has the power to shape the entire world's economy—jobs, businesses, factories, farms, and banks all around the world.

WORLD WAR I

World War I began in 1914. It lasted for three long years. It was terrible. Many, many people died. Europe was filled with barbed-wire fences, mines, trenches, and poison gas.

Two sides were fighting in this war. On one side were the Central Powers. They were Germany, Austria-Hungary, the Ottoman Empire, and Bulgaria. On the other side were the Allied forces. They were the United States, the United Kingdom, France, Belgium, Russia, and others.

The two sides faced off across the Western Front. This was a line drawn down Europe. Lots of people died fighting on the Western Front. Some **civilians** got caught in between.

At first the United States was not involved with the war. Neither side was really wining or losing during those first couple years. Men were dying on both sides, but nothing was being accomplished. Then the United States joined the Allies. That changed things. American troops added energy to the Allies.

The United States sent more and more soldiers to Europe. Pretty soon the Allies were winning battles. And they were winning the war.

World War I poster

Civilians are the ordinary people, not members of the military or the government.

In 1918, the German leader stepped down. Then the Germans accepted a ceasefire. The war was over!

RECOVERING

In 1918, the United States President was Woodrow Wilson. He announced the end of the war to the United States. Then he started thinking about how to rebuild Europe. The war had destroyed a lot of things.

President Wilson didn't think that the winners should take revenge on the losers. They shouldn't still be angry about the war. Then Europe would have peace.

The trenches of World War I

11

The U.S. troops prepare to join the fighting.

But people were still angry. The Allies wanted to punish Germany especially. They wanted Germany to pay billions of dollars to make up for the war. Germans couldn't afford that. They had to rebuild their country.

The Allies also wanted Germany to get rid of its weapons, so that it would not be able to attack other nations again. So Germans destroyed their guns, trains, planes, and submarines. Germany had no more power and it was poor.

Meanwhile, President Wilson wanted to start something called the League of Nations. The League of Nations would be an organization of all the countries of the world. He thought it would prevent a war from happening again. Countries could talk about their problems instead of fight over them.

Woodrow Wilson

Americans didn't really like the League of Nations. They didn't want other countries having any say over the decisions the United States made. The United States didn't end up joining the League of Nations, even though it was the American President's idea.

GOOD TIMES AND BAD TIMES

After World War I, the United States focused on its own affairs. Lots of things happened after the war. Not all of them were good.

During World War I, a group called the **communists** took over Russia. The communists believed that the government should own all property, like land. Everyone would work together to make life good for all.

The United States is **capitalist**. Individual people make choices about their property. Americans didn't like communists because they believed something different than capitalists.

Some people in the United States thought that communists might cause problems here. They wanted to crush any communist ideas. The government started spying on people they suspected might be communists. They sent some people to jail.

Communist star

Communists are people that believe the government should control all of a nation's wealth and distribute it fairly. If communism worked the way it was intended, there would be no very poor people and no very rich people. Instead, everyone would share the nation's money. Communism hasn't very often worked out, though, since it makes the government very strong and takes away power from individual workers.

Capitalist is a word that has to do with "capitalism," which is a very different system for handling a country's money. Under capitalism, the government has very little control over how money is spent. Instead, individual workers and businesses control their own money.

Guglielmo Marconi,
radio inventor

At the same time, the 1920s were called the Roaring Twenties. People were trying to have a good time after the war. Movies became popular. At first, they were silent— they didn't have sound. Then filmmakers figured out how to add sound to the movies. Jazz music was also big. Jazz has African American roots, but in the Roaring Twenties, everyone was enjoying it. People could listen to jazz on the radio, another popular piece of entertainment.

Things we take for granted today were new in the 1920s. Electricity in homes was a big deal. Not many people had electricity at home before World War I. Afterward, more homes were powered with electricity.

Fashions during the Roaring Twenties

Cars became cheaper. Ordinary people could buy cars. That changed the way we get to work, how we take vacations, and what the landscape of the United States looked like.

People moved out of cities. Now they could drive to work. But they could live outside of the city. They moved to suburbs, which were brand new back then.

The United States was feeling pretty good about itself. It had proven it was a world power during World War I. And now many Americans were getting rich and enjoying themselves.

Herbert Hoover became president of the United States in 1929.

Chapter Two
THE GREAT DEPRESSION

The good times didn't last long. In 1929, the Great Depression hit America. This was a hard time for just about everyone. The Great Depression affected Americans of all sorts. It affected people all over the world.

THE BEGINNING

At the beginning of the 1920s, the people who were having a good time in America wanted to buy all these new things that were becoming popular. But they didn't always have the money to buy them. Instead, they used something called credit. People could buy something now. Then they could pay for it later. They were in debt until they paid.

Individual people did this. So did companies. To pay their debts, companies offered stocks to people. Buying a stock is like buying a tiny piece of a company.

If the company did well, then people with stocks made money. If it did poorly, stock-holders would lose money. The stock market was the place where all these sales took place. The stock market became pretty popular in the 1920s. People were excited about getting rich by buying and selling stock.

But people didn't always have money to buy the stocks either. They used credit to buy stocks.

So now lots of people and companies were in debt. No one had any money to pay for anything. But they kept on buying.

Something had to give. First, houses got cheaper. People started buying less. But the stock market did better and better.

Then the prices of stocks started falling. They kept falling. People panicked. They sold all their stocks. When they sold all their stocks, the value of the stocks dropped. It was a vicious circle. In the end, everything came crashing down.

DARK YEARS

Now things were bad. People lost all their money. No one could afford to buy anything. So companies had to close down. They fired thousands of people.

The Great Depression lasted through all of the 1930s. It affected other countries too. The United States economy was tied to other countries' economies. If the United States did badly, so did other nations.

Crowds mill around the New York Stock Exchange on October 24, 1929.

18

An abandoned dust bowl era homestead on the northern Colorado plains.

THE DUST BOWL

Beginning in 1931, severe drought (a long period with no rain) in the Midwest and southern plains made the Great Depression even worse. Farmland turned to dust. Crops shriveled, animals died, and windstorms blew the farmland away. The area was called the Dust Bowl.

Many farm families had to move to the cities to find work. Others streamed west to get to farms where they could work again. Eight years later, rain fell and the Dust Bowl was over.

Franklin D. Roosevelt

Without money, people couldn't pay for homes or for food. It was a hard life for lots of Americans.

A NEW LEADER

During the Great Depression, Americans weren't very happy with the President, Herbert Hoover. They thought he hadn't done enough to prevent the Great Depression.

Franklin D. Roosevelt ran for President. He promised to help people. He was elected president in 1932. But the Great Depression got worse and worse.

Roosevelt came up with a plan to help the country. It was called the New Deal. It put people back to work. It built lots of buildings, roads, and bridges. It made laws so that something like this wouldn't happen again.

Some people liked the New Deal. It was helping the country. Some didn't. They thought it gave the President and the government had too much power. They thought it took away America's capitalism (the money system that gives power to people and businesses) and made the country a little more like communism (the money system where the government controls wealth).

Through it all President Roosevelt held "fireside chats." He would talk to Americans through the radio. He tried to comfort them. He also explained what was going on in the United States.

For a while, there was no end in sight to the Great Depression. But then things changed. Unfortunately, what ended the Great Depression was another war.

President Roosevelt doing one of his famous "fireside chats."

THEY (WHO) SEEK TO ESTABLISH
SYSTEMS OF GOVERNMENT BASED ON
THE REGIMENTATION OF ALL HUMAN
BEINGS BY A HANDFUL OF INDIVIDUAL
RULERS... CALL THIS A NEW ORDER.
IT IS NOT NEW AND IT IS NOT ORDER.

Franklin Delano Roosevelt Memorial in Washington, D. C.

A NEW KIND OF FIRST LADY

Eleanor Roosevelt was the President's wife. She changed the role of First Lady. Before, the First Lady was just the President's wife. Eleanor was much more than that. As First Lady, she traveled on fact-finding missions for the President. She talked to newspapers, gave radio addresses, and wrote a daily newspaper column. She constantly spoke up for poor people and their rights.

World War II poster

Chapter Three
ANOTHER WORLD WAR

People thought that the world war they had just fought would be the last one. No one wanted a repeat.

But it happened again. World War I had involved mostly only Europe and North America, but World War II really was a world war. This time people all over the world got involved.

Just like in World War I, there were the Allied forces. The United States, Britain, and others were on the Allied side. On the other side were the Axis Powers. That included Germany and Japan.

STORM CLOUDS

The war took a while to get started. While the United States was struggling through the Great Depression, things were happening in Germany as well. The country was still dealing with the effects of World War I. It didn't have much money. And other countries looked down on it.

Germans wanted someone to fix their country. They wanted to feel proud of their nation again. A man named Adolph Hitler promised to do the job. The people who supported him were called Nazis.

Hitler thought that the best Germans were those he called "Aryans." These were people with light skin. They had blonde or brown hair. They had light-colored eyes. He thought these people were better than everyone else.

Hitler and the Nazi flag

Hitler blamed other people for Germany's problems. He blamed Jews. He blamed communists. He blamed gypsies and homosexuals. But not the Aryans.

Soon, Hitler was very powerful. He controlled the whole government. But Hitler wanted to control more than just Germany. He wanted to take over Europe.

First, he took over nearby countries. The rest of the world just let him. People didn't want another war.

More problems were going on in other parts of the world too. In Asia, Japan was getting more powerful. Its army was getting bigger. It invaded China. The Japanese army killed people and bombed Chinese cities.

ALL OUT WAR

Germany invaded Poland next, in 1939. Finally, the world responded. England and France declared war on Germany. World War II began.

The Germans looked unstoppable. Hitler took over more and more countries. He even defeated France in less than a year. Now it was mostly Britain all by itself against Germany.

26

So far, the United States didn't want to fight in the war. Americans wanted to stay out of what was going on in Europe and in Asia.

But they did take sides. Japan kept on taking over countries in Asia. The United States decided to stop selling oil and metal to Japan. Without oil and metal, Japan couldn't keep attacking other countries.

THE UNITED STATES JOINS THE WAR

The Japanese were mad. They took action. On December 7, 1941, Japanese planes flew to Hawaii. They aimed for Pearl Harbor. The United States kept war boats and weapons there.

The planes started bombing Pearl Harbor. Japan also attacked United States forces in other parts of the Pacific Ocean. Americans couldn't ignore the war anymore. Now they were being attacked!

THE WAR AT HOME

Hawaii was the only part of the United States the fighting ever actually reached. No one ever fought on the mainland. But that doesn't mean that the war didn't affect Americans.

World War II was the end of the Great Depression in the United States. Now the United States needed people to make war goods. Workers flooded into factories to make guns and tanks and other things. People had jobs again.

The government controlled the prices of things. They **rationed** out food and gas. The United States needed enough of those things for the war. Americans couldn't use them all at home.

When something is **rationed**, it's passed out in small portions to the people who want it. For example, if your mother rationed the cereal, your family might get just one bowl of cereal a day. Once you had used up your ration for the day, you wouldn't be able to get more cereal until the next day. The rationing during World War II worked like that. People could only buy so much food and gasoline at a time. It didn't matter if they used it up and needed more. They had to wait until it was their turn to buy more.

Woman factory worker.

Now there actually weren't *enough* workers anymore. So companies had to find new people to hire so that America's factories could make the things the war needed. Most men were in the army—so companies hired women.

Lots of women went to work in factories and other places. It was the first time that some women had even thought of working outside the home. This was a big change!

President Roosevelt kept being President. He was elected four times! That meant he led the country longer than any other U.S. President in history. Now, Presidents can only now be elected two times (for eight years).

During his fourth term, Roosevelt died. His Vice President Harry S. Truman took over. Truman had to lead the country through the end of the war.

THE AMERICAN CONCENTRATION CAMPS

Hitler put the Jews and other people he didn't like in terrible places called concentration camps. Millions of people died there.

During World War II, the United States had its own concentration camps called internment camps. After the bombing of Pearl Harbor, Americans didn't trust Japanese people. They thought that they might side with Japan and hurt the United States. Really, it was just racism. Other Americans didn't like Japanese or Japanese-Americans.

The government decided to round up thousands of Japanese-Americans. They were forced to live in camps. These camps weren't as bad as the Nazi concentration camps. The point wasn't to kill everyone in them. It was just to keep them separate. But they were still horrible and cruel.

Some Italian- and German-Americans were also put in camps, since the United States was fighting Italy and Germany. Italians and Germans not in camps couldn't travel freely or carry cameras.

War does terrible things!

THE WAR DRAGS ON

The war went on for many years. No one knew who would win. First one side would win a battle. Then the other side.

In Europe, Hitler and the Nazis were doing terrible things. Hitler wanted to get rid of all those people he said caused Germany's problems. He forced them into concentration camps where he killed millions of people. Today, this is known as the Holocaust.

The Nazis especially hated the Jews. They also killed gypsies, gay people, and other people who believed in certain religions. The Nazis killed 12 million people by the end of the Holocaust.

However, slowly the tide started turning against Germany. The Germans lost some battles. The Allies were beating the Germans down.

THE END IS NEAR

The Allied attack on German-controlled France was called D-Day. Lots of Allied troops landed on the coast of France. They fought with the Germans. Many people died. But the Allies won. They broke through the German army and freed France.

Eventually the Allies captured Berlin, the capital of Germany. And then Germany surrendered in May of 1945.

But there was still the war in Asia. The United States was slowly winning, but the Japanese kept fighting. People thought the war might drag on forever.

But it wouldn't. The United States was creating a new weapon. It was the atomic bomb. President Truman had to decide whether to use it or not. He gave Japan a warning. They didn't listen.

The United States dropped an atomic bomb on the city of Hiroshima. Eighty thousand people died instantly. More died later from **radiation** poisoning. Still Japan didn't give up. The United States dropped another atomic bomb on Nagasaki. It killed even more people.

Finally Japan surrendered. No one was fighting any more and the war was over. Now it was time to rebuild.

Atomic bombing
of Nagasaki on
August 9, 1945.

Radiation is the energy that something releases. The energy from the atom bomb was very bad for people's bodies. It caused cancer and made them very sick.

Atomic bomb test.

Chapter Four
FIGHTING SUPERPOWERS

For a very long time, Western Europe had the most power of anywhere on Earth. Countries like France and England controlled everything else. Now it was different.

World War II had destroyed many Western European countries. They had to start over. Two other countries took over as the most powerful. Those were the United States and the Soviet Union. The Soviet Union was made up of Russia and some other countries nearby.

The two countries had both been Allies. But they didn't really get along. The Soviet Union was communist. And most Americans didn't like communists.

RECOVERING

The United States and the Soviet Union each helped Europe out after the war. The Soviets took control of the eastern part of Europe. The United States helped the western part.

President Truman came up with the Truman Doctrine. This said that the United States would basically help any country that was fighting communism. America would give these countries money and weapons. The United States ended up helping out Greece and Turkey.

THE BIRTH OF THE UNITED NATIONS

When the League of Nations failed to stop World War II, it ceased to exist. But the world needed another organization like it. The United Nations (UN) officially was born on October 24, 1945. China, France, the Soviet Union, the United Kingdom, and the United States, along with other member states, signed the agreement. The UN still exists today.

The United States also came up with the Marshall Plan. This gave out money to countries in Western Europe. Britain, France, and others had to rebuild. Buildings were gone. People were sick or dead. Farms were destroyed. There was a lot to do.

THE COLD WAR

The United States and the Soviet Union soon entered another war. But there wasn't really any direct fighting in this war. Armies didn't face off against each other. Guns weren't fired and bombs weren't dropped.

Both countries wanted to be the only powerful one. They didn't want the other one to have so much power.

Each tried to build nuclear weapons. The United States made the first ones. But the Soviets weren't far behind. Soon both countries had very dangerous weapons.

People were afraid of nuclear war. If anything happened, one country could bomb the other. Then that one would fight back with its own bombs. The world would be destroyed in the process. No one could win.

MORE FIGHTING

Meanwhile, in China, there was a civil war. (A civil war is when two parts of the same

Korean civilians

country fight against each other.) Communist forces took over. China was now communist. So was nearby North Korea. The United States was worried even more countries would become communist.

In 1950, North Korea invaded South Korea. South Korea wasn't communist. The United States wanted to keep it that way. The United States army sent forces to stop the communists. China sent its army to fight for the North Koreans.

Neither side really won. They fought for three years but nothing changed. A lot of people died, though.

Communists had also taken over Vietnam, another country in Asia. A man named Ho Chi-Minh was the leader there. He was communist.

The Soviet Union and China fought on the same side as Ho Chi-Minh. The United States fought to keep Vietnam from becoming communist. Eventually the country was split in half, like Korea. The north was communist. The south wasn't.

THE MCCARTHY ERA

One senator really wanted to get rid of communism in the United States. That was Senator Joseph McCarthy. He fired government employees if they were suspected of liking communism. His fear infected U.S. society as a whole. Libraries threw out books with ties to communism. Actors, artists, professors, and others who agreed with communism couldn't find jobs. Some high schools even required students to sign loyalty oaths to the U.S. government before they could receive their diplomas.

Joseph McCarthy

But people in Vietnam wanted to be a whole country. Lots of people agreed with Ho Chi-Minh. Some people in the south called the Vietcong fought to become one country.

The United States sent more and more soldiers to Vietnam. The Vietnam War lasted for a very long time. In 1968, the North Vietnamese started winning.

Back in the United States, people were angry. They wanted the war to end. There were huge **protests**. Finally, the war ended in 1975.

CUBA

During the 1960s, the United States was also worried about another country. A communist called Fidel Castro had taken over Cuba. Cuba is an island to the south of the United States.

The United States helped a small force invade Cuba. President John F. Kennedy was in charge. The force landed at the Bay of Pigs in 1961. It was a complete disaster. Then Cuba asked the Soviet Union for help.

The next year the Soviets started building missile bases in Cuba, places where rockets could be shot. The rocket would be able to launch nuclear weapons right at the United States. For a while, the world held its breath. Everyone knew there could be a nuclear war.

President Kennedy talked to the Soviets. The United States and the Soviet Union agreed to a **compromise**. Nobody would use any nuclear weapons.

Protests are when people speak out against the government. Sometimes protests are peaceful and no one gets hurt. Sometimes they can become violent.

A **compromise** is when two sides that are arguing both agree to give in a little bit and meet in the middle.

PRESIDENTS

There were several American Presidents during the Cold War. After Harry Truman left the White House, President Dwight Eisenhower took over. He had been a general during World War II.

Then after Eisenhower came John F. Kennedy. He was also called JFK. He was a very popular president. He wanted Americans to think positively and to do great things. He also helped create the space program that sent people into space.

Millions were shocked when a gunman killed JFK in 1963. His Vice President, Lyndon Johnson, took over. Johnson was only President for one term after that.

Then came Richard Nixon. He was a **controversial** president. He promised to end the Vietnam War, so he got elected. He didn't end it. He actually sent more troops to Vietnam.

Nixon ended up **resigning** as president. During his reelection, he did some illegal things. He was afraid he wouldn't be reelected. He had people break into his opponents' headquarters in the Watergate Hotel in Washington, D.C.

Nixon got in a lot of trouble for that. It was called the Watergate **scandal**. Before he could be fired, he resigned. His Vice President, Gerald Ford, became President then.

LOTS OF CHANGE

Besides wars, other things were going on during this time. Lots of changes happened after World War II.

If something is **controversial,** people don't agree about it. It causes arguments both for and against.

Resigning means officially quitting a job.

A **scandal** is something bad that everyone talks about.

Young people especially did things differently. They listened to different music. They challenged **social norms** they had been taught. They wore different clothes. They grew long hair and beards.

The Civil Rights Movement also happened during this time. A lot of people spoke out to make sure all Americans were treated equally. African Americans especially had faced hatred and discrimination. So did women.

Martin Luther King, Jr. was the most famous civil rights leader. He urged all people to fight for African Americans' rights. He said black Americans should be treated just the same as everyone else.

He won the Nobel Peace Prize for his work. This is a very important prize that's given to people who have done a lot to bring peace to the world. But not everyone agreed with King. Some people who were racist hated him. They didn't like that he was changing America. One of his enemies shot and killed him in 1968.

Lots of things were going on in the 1950s, '60s, and '70s. Some of these were good things. Some of them were terrible things. Through it all, the United States started looking a lot more like it does today.

Martin Luther King, Jr.

Social norms are the accepted way of doing things, the way people have always done things.

39

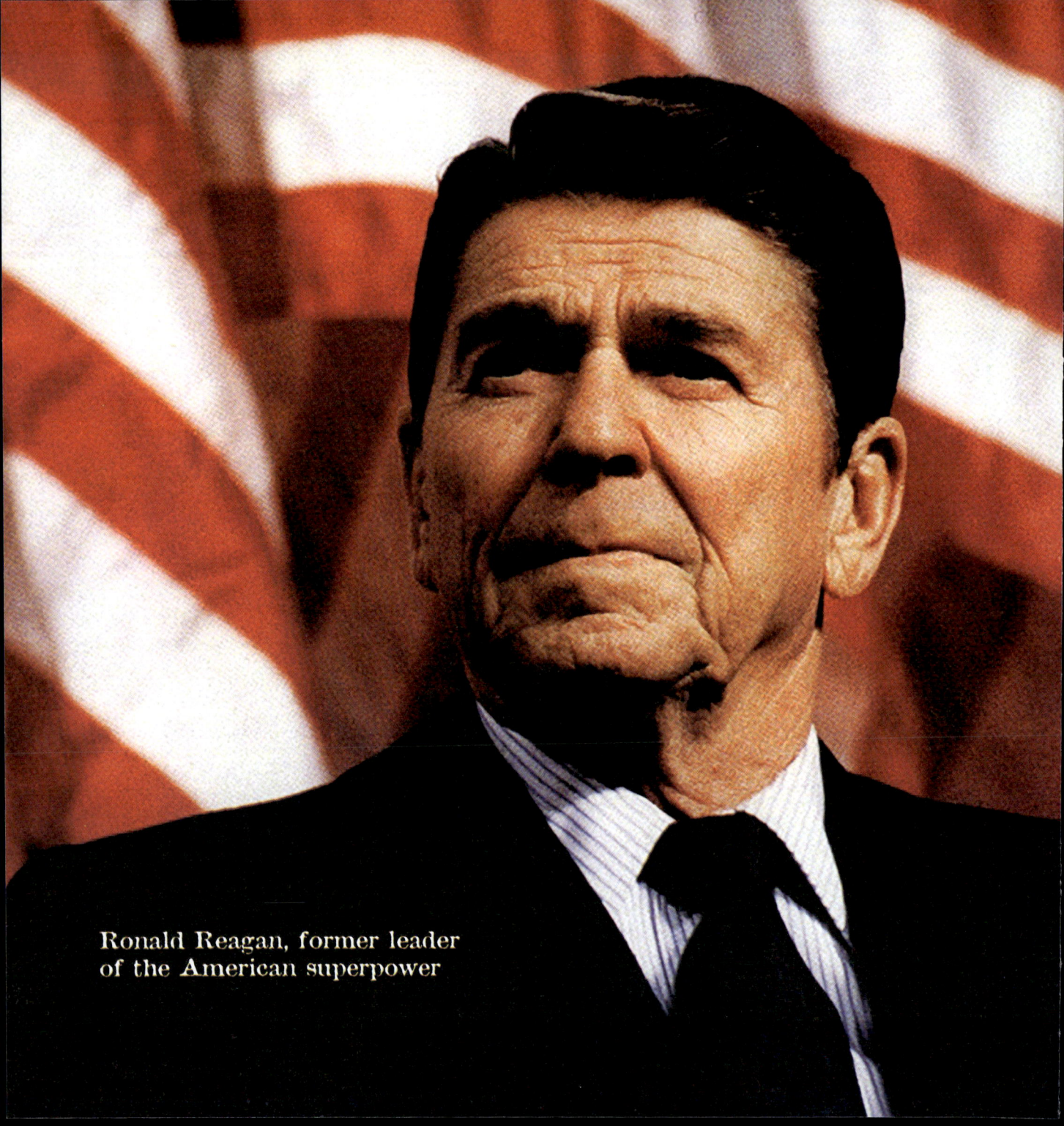

Ronald Reagan, former leader
of the American superpower

Chapter Five
LAST SUPERPOWER STANDING

By the 1980s, the Cold War was ending. The Soviet Union started getting weaker. But the United States stayed strong.

THE SOVIETS BACK DOWN

The Soviet government made a lot of mistakes. It scared people and treated them badly. It took over other countries that didn't want to be under their control.

In 1985, Mikhail Gorbachev became the leader of the Soviet Union. He decided that communism wasn't really working. The Soviet Union was not doing very well.

Gorbachev wanted to make the Soviet Union's economy grow. He made some changes. He worked with United States President Ronald Reagan. So much happened that communism came crashing down.

The Soviet Union disappeared. This gave many countries their freedom. All of a sudden, there were a dozen new countries that used to be part of the Soviet Union. The Cold War was over.

STAYING STRONG

The United States was the only superpower left. There was no other strong country to rival it.

THE BERLIN WALL

The Berlin Wall was built to cut Germany in half after World War II. On the west side, the United States had a lot of power. On the east side, the Soviets had the power.

West Germany did a lot better after the war. East Germany got poorer. The wall kept families and friends apart too. No one could cross.

Germans hated the wall. Eventually, the wall guards started tearing down the wall. Lots of regular people helped too. The Soviet Union couldn't do anything to stop them. It symbolized the end of the Cold War.

But with all that power comes the choice of how to use it. Some people have not been happy with how the United States has used its power.

There were more wars after the Cold War. The first one was the Gulf War. When Iraq invaded Kuwait, The United States went to war to defend Kuwait. It was a short war. It only lasted about seven months. The United States won, but a lot of Iraqi people died.

Meanwhile, at home in America, the economy was in trouble. In the 1980s, things were hard for a lot of people. Some people didn't have jobs. The government was spending too much money. It wasn't as bad as the Great Depression though.

President George Bush tried to fix things. He wasn't very successful. Americans voted Bill Clinton into office instead. The 1990s ended up being very prosperous. Now people had jobs, and they were making money. The economy was healthier.

MORE PRESIDENTS

President Clinton was very popular for most of his time as president. However, he did get into trouble during his last couple years.

People found out that Clinton had been too close to an **intern** in the White House. Then he had lied about it.

The government investigated. Congress decided to **impeach** him. Clinton ended up not being convicted of doing anything wrong. He finished up his term as President.

Former United States President, Bill Clinton

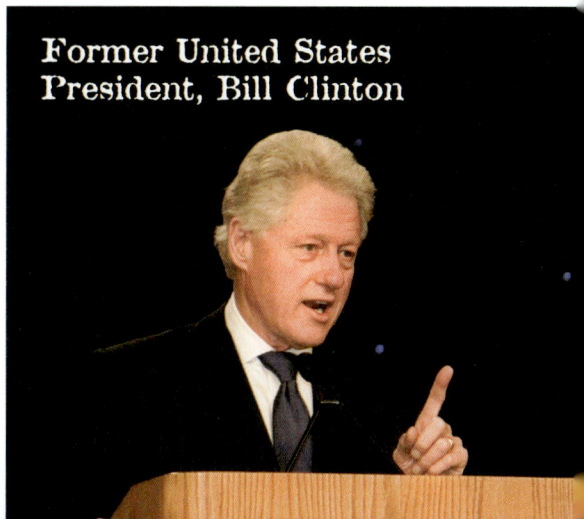

An **intern** is a student being trained on the job.

To **impeach** means to charge an official of doing something wrong.

43

Then there was a presidential election in 2000. It was very close. Clinton's Vice President Al Gore ran against George W. Bush. Bush was the son of the former President George Bush.

Bush ended up becoming President. Not everyone was happy, though. Bush's election divided many Americans.

9/11

Life in American changed hugely one day in September of 2001. That day, a plane flew into a tower of the World Trade Center in New York City. People couldn't believe it. They didn't know what had happened. They thought it was an accident.

Then a second plane crashed into the other tower. This clearly wasn't an accident. Pretty soon, Americans found out that terrorists had hijacked four planes. One flew into the Pentagon in Washington, DC. The other crashed in a field in Pennsylvania.

September 11 shocked the world. Thousands of people died. The United States was not as safe as people had thought.

The government soon figured out who was responsible. It was group called al Qaeda. A man named Osama bin Laden was in charge. Al Qaeda was an extreme Islamic group.

September 11th Memorial

This group didn't like the United States getting involved in the Middle East.

Bin Laden was hiding in Afghanistan. But Afghanistan refused to hand him over to the United States. A group called the Taliban ruled the country.

The United States sent soldiers to Afghanistan. The goal was to get rid of the Taliban and to kill bin Laden. This was the start of the "War on Terror."

Two months later, the Taliban were gone. But bin Laden was still on the loose.

ANOTHER WAR

The United States was already involved with one war in Afghanistan. Then it started another one in Iraq.

President Bush decided that Iraq must have dangerous weapons. He was afraid that Iraq would use them against the United States. He sent in the military to find the weapons.

No one found any weapons. But the United States kept fighting. President Bush told Saddam Hussein, the leader of Iraq, to quit and leave. Hussein was a **dictator**. He didn't leave. And the United States kept fighting.

In 2003, President Bush declared that the United States won the war in Iraq. But fighting didn't end. It lasted for a long time. Many people didn't like Americans being there. They formed groups to fight them. Meanwhile, lots of people died on both sides.

By the end of the twentieth century, there were good things and bad things going on in the United States. Lots of people were focusing on the two wars being fought. But the economy was doing well. People were living their lives.

And the United States was still the strongest country in the world.

A **dictator** is a ruler who has all the power.

FIND OUT MORE

In Books

Adams, Simon. *World War I.* New York: DK Publishing, Inc., 2007.

Brown, Don. *America Under Attack: September 11, 2001.* New York: Roaring Brook, 2011.

Panchyk, Richard. *World War II: A History with 21 Activities.* Chicago, Ill.: Chicago Review Press, Inc., 2002.

Taylor, David. *The Cold War (Twentieth Century Perspectives).* Chicago, Ill.: Heinemann-Raintree, 2001.

On the Internet

Cold War Museum
www.coldwar.org

Presidents
www.whitehouse.gov/about/presidents

September
www.classbrain.com/artfree/publish/cat_index_17.shtml

World War I
www.socialstudiesforkids.com/subjects/worldwari.htm

INDEX

ABOUT THE AUTHOR
AND THE CONSULTANT

Victor South is a freelance author from New York State. He grew up reading the stories that helped shape America. He is excited about the opportunity to share these stories with a new generation of children.

Dr. Jack N. Rakove is a professor of history and American studies at Stanford University, where he is director of American studies. The winner of the 1997 Pulitzer Prize in history, Dr. Rakove is the author of *The Unfinished Election of 2000*, *Constitutional Culture and Democratic Rule*, and *James Madison and the Creation of the American Republic*. He is also the president of the Society for the History of the Early American Republic.